W9-CZW-650

APR - - 2013

Learning About the Digestive and Excretory Systems

by Susan Dudley Gold

Enslow Publishers, Inc.
40 Industrial Road
Box 398
Berkeley Heights, NJ 07922
USA

http://www.enslow.com

Dedicated to my grandmother,
Ruth Goff Walton

Original edition published as *The Digestive and Excretory Systems* in 2004.

Library of Congress Cataloging-in-Publication Data

Gold, Susan Dudley.
  Learning about the digestive and excretory systems / Susan Dudley Gold.
      p. cm. — (Learning about the human body systems)
  Summary: "Learn how these remarkable systems work together to bring us life-giving nutrients and rid our bodies of waste"— Provided by publisher.
  Includes bibliographical references and index.
  ISBN 978-0-7660-4157-8
  1. Digestive organs—Juvenile literature. 2. Urinary organs—Juvenile literature. I. Title.
  QP145.G656 2013
  612.3—dc23

                                                                                2012011100

Future editions:
Paperback ISBN 978-1-4644-0235-7
ePUB ISBN 978-1-4645-1154-7
PDF ISBN 978-1-4646-1154-4

Printed in the United States of America

082012 Lake Book Manufacturing, Inc., Melrose Park, IL

10 9 8 7 6 5 4 3 2 1

To Our Readers: We have done our best to make sure all Internet addresses in this book were active and appropriate when we went to press. However, the author and the publisher have no control over and assume no liability for the material available on those Internet sites or on other Web sites they may link to. Any comments or suggestions can be sent by e-mail to comments@enslow.com or to the address on the back cover.

♻ Enslow Publishers, Inc., is committed to printing our books on recycled paper. The paper in every book contains 10% to 30% post-consumer waste (PCW). The cover board on the outside of each book contains 100% PCW. Our goal is to do our part to help young people and the environment too!

Photo Credits: © Life Art, Williams & Wilkins, pp. 4 (left), 4 (right), 11, 12, 15, 16, 19, 21, 23, 26, 31, 37, 38, 39; Shutterstock.com, pp. 1, 7, 34, 36.

Cover Photo: Shutterstock.com

Contents

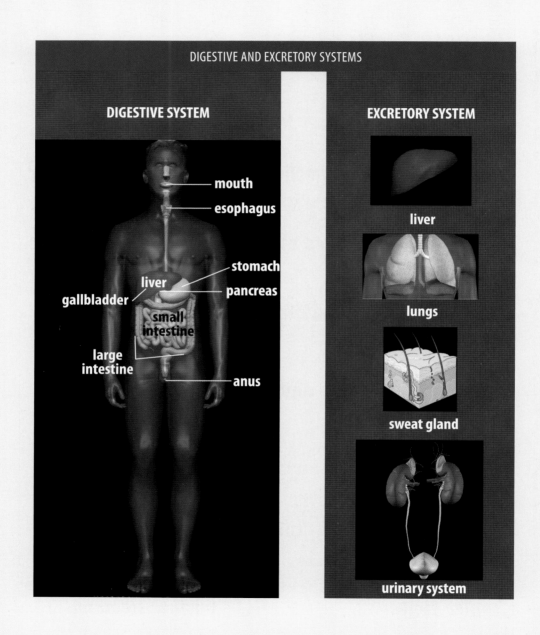

DIGESTIVE AND EXCRETORY SYSTEMS

DIGESTIVE SYSTEM

- mouth
- esophagus
- stomach
- liver
- pancreas
- gallbladder
- small intestine
- large intestine
- anus

EXCRETORY SYSTEM

liver

lungs

sweat gland

urinary system

What Are the Digestive and Excretory Systems?

Mary's mouth waters when she thinks of chocolate cheesecake. By 10 A.M. Ben's stomach growls if he doesn't eat a snack.

We all need food. Food gives us energy. It provides the fuel our bodies need to perform the tasks that keep us alive. But our bodies can't use food until it is processed—broken down into tiny parts.

Putting gas into a car without an engine would be useless. Likewise, without a digestive system, we would starve to death even if we ate six meals a day. The digestive system dissolves the food we eat and extracts nutrients from it. The bloodstream then carries these nutrients, with their precious cargo of energy, to the rest of the body.

The human body depends on the digestive system for the energy necessary for life. From tiny cells to a thirty-foot tube to

5

organs the size of a fist, each part of the system plays an important role in keeping us healthy.

Just one swallow of food sets the digestive system into action. Every bite we eat must be mashed, crushed, chopped into tiny pieces, turned to mush, and broken down into molecules before it can do us any good. Nutrients must be processed and stored. Water must be absorbed. Vitamins must be dissolved.

After a full meal, a person may doze. But the internal body does not rest. In fact, this is its busiest time. Food quickly enters the stomach after being chewed and softened by the teeth and the mouth. For the next twenty-four hours or so, the body will process the food, extract the nutrients, and expel the waste. The stomach works on the food, then passes it to the small intestines for further processing. Here the food finally becomes small enough for the body to absorb it.

The body must also get rid of waste products. The digestive system separates out wastes from food and expels them. Other wastes, the result of chemical reactions in the body, are disposed of through the excretory system. Chemical reactions allow us to breathe, bring water into our systems, and do many other activities that keep us alive. The excretory system gets rid of the waste products from each of these activities. Part of the excretory system's job is to regulate the amount of salt and water in the body. In addition, the system expels carbon dioxide, a waste gas exhaled through the lungs. The system also gets rid of waste materials that exit the body in the form of sweat.

When working well, the two systems are remarkably efficient. Very little is wasted. The kidneys filter about 200 quarts (190 liters) of liquid a day. Only about 2 quarts (1.9 liters) leave the body as urine.[1] The digestive system processes an average of 8 to 10 quarts (7.5 to 9.5 liters) of food and liquid daily. Of that amount, only about 3 to 8 ounces (.89 to 2.36 deciliters) are ejected as feces.[2] Feces is the solid waste eliminated during a bowel movement.

The digestive system transforms the food we eat into energy our bodies can use.

One little glitch in either system, however, can cause big problems. For example, diarrhea occurs when something irritates the intestines. This signals the system to empty the intestines. The food passes through too quickly to allow nutrients and water to be absorbed by the body. A person, especially a young child, can die from dehydration—lack of fluids—if diarrhea continues too long.

The digestive and the excretory systems take the food we eat through a marvelous maze. By the time it reaches the maze's end, Ben's mid-morning snack has given him the energy to chase a fly ball. Along the way, the systems have cleansed his blood and provided the nutrients necessary for life itself.

Chapter 2

Members of the Team

The digestive system and the excretory system work hand in hand to keep the body healthy, nourished, and cleansed. The two systems depend on many body parts to assist them. Organs such as the pancreas, the liver, and the gallbladder help out. Nerves, muscles, and **hormones** also get in on the act. This team performs the many complex tasks involved in digestion and excretion.

Digestive System

The digestive system runs an amazingly efficient food-processing plant. The system operates in the gastrointestinal or **digestive tract**. This long tube runs from the mouth to the anus. With its twists and turns, it extends about thirty feet (nine meters). Food travels through the digestive tract and is processed along the way. The tract includes the mouth, the esophagus, the stomach, the small and large intestines, and the anus. Other organs help in the food-processing work.

Along the walls of the digestive tract are layers of smooth muscle. A thick, moist membrane called the mucosa coats the inside of the tract. The mucosa has three sublayers and several tasks. It secretes **mucus**, a thick, slippery fluid that acts like oil in a machine to keep the entire system lubricated. It also releases **enzymes** and hormones that help digest the food we eat. An enzyme is a **protein** that speeds up chemical reactions. Hormones carry instructions from one part of the body to another. The mucosa also absorbs digested nutrients and returns them to the bloodstream.

Like an assembly line, the digestive tract has "workers" all along the way. From the moment food enters the mouth to the time waste leaves the body through the anus, these working body parts mash the food, grind it, soften it, dissolve it, and pass it along to the next workstation. Strong bands of muscle, called **sphincters**, separate the work stations. They operate like one-way doors that open only when pushed. These muscular valves help separate the parts of the digestive tract. This prevents harsh substances in one chamber from harming the next chamber in line.

MOUTH. The mouth has the equipment needed to mash and soften food. This gets that apple or that cheeseburger ready for the trek through the digestive tract. Three sets of **glands** in the mouth release a watery substance called **saliva**. This moistens the food and makes it easier to chew.

Teeth crush the food. Tough enamel coats these hard, rigid structures. Gums of soft tissue act as shock absorbers when the teeth bite and chew. The jawbone anchors the teeth and allows them to move up and down.

9

When we chop onions, we select a special knife designed for that chore. Another type of knife makes it easy to slice bread. Our teeth serve us in a similar way. We use our front teeth—sharp incisors shaped like chisels—to bite into an apple. If the steak is tough, pointed canines rip off a piece of the meat. Farther back in the mouth, premolars with two ridges crush the food into a mushy mass. The largest and strongest teeth, the molars in the back of the mouth, grind food into even smaller and finer bits.

The tongue moves food around in the mouth, pushing it between the teeth. The tongue has thousands of tiny bumps called papillae. Many of the papillae contain tiny taste buds that let us taste food. These taste buds send signals to the brain, which interprets the reports. Some taste buds detect sweet tastes, while others sense sour or bitter tastes.

ESOPHAGUS. The swallowed food enters the esophagus, a tube about 10 inches (25 centimeters) long. This tube runs from the back of the mouth into the stomach. It is lined with two layers of strong muscles that push the food on its way. The outer muscles run lengthwise up and down the throat. The inner muscles form circles around the inside of the esophagus. At the bottom of the esophagus, a thick band of muscle—called the cardiac sphincter—opens to allow food into the stomach. The band then closes quickly so that stomach acid will not escape and damage the esophagus.

STOMACH. The real work of the body's processing plant begins in the stomach. Shaped like a fat letter J, the stomach consists of three layers of smooth muscle. This stretchy bag can expand to hold almost a quart (about one liter) of food at a time.

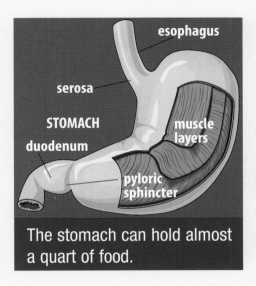

The stomach can hold almost a quart of food.

Several layers of tissue cover the stomach muscles. The submucosa, a layer of loose tissue, carries blood vessels and nerves that connect to the stomach. A thin layer of tissue called **serosa** coats the outer stomach and protects it.

Like the cardiac sphincter at the top of the stomach opening, another band of muscle blocks off the lower opening. This band, called the pyloric sphincter, separates the stomach from the small intestine. It opens just enough to allow small portions of digested food into the intestines. The band also protects the stomach from **bile**—a thick, yellowish-green liquid made in the liver—that might leak from where it is stored in the small intestine.

SMALL INTESTINE. The small intestine looks like a garden hose coiled inside the body. It is attached to the stomach on one end and the large intestine on the other. This tubing is about 18 to 23 feet (5.5 to 7 meters) long and an inch (2.5 centimeters) wide. It consists of four layers. Like the stomach, the intestine—with the exception of the duodenum—is coated with serosa. The muscularis, a thick layer of muscle, surrounds the submucosa, where nerves and blood vessels are located. In the inner section of the tubing lies the mucosa. Within the mucosa, millions of **villi**—structures shaped like tiny fingers—stand ready to absorb nutrients.

The small intestine has three sections. The duodenum, the smallest segment, connects to the stomach. It is shaped like a letter C and takes up about the first 12 inches (30 centimeters) of the small intestine. The next section of small intestine, the jejunum, forms a coil that is about 5 feet (1.5 meters) long. The

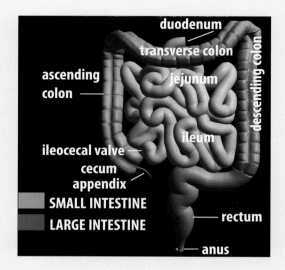

third section is the ileum. This part measures about 8 feet (2.5 meters). Another sphincter called the ileocecal valve lies between the small intestine and the large intestine.

LARGE INTESTINE. The large intestine is a tube divided into segments. It looks like a large vacuum hose framed around the small intestine. The large intestine is about 5 feet (1.5 meters) long and 2.5 inches (6.4 centimeters) in diameter. Inside the large intestine, the structure is the same as that of the small intestine.

The cecum, a small pouch of tissue, is located at the point where the small intestine joins the large intestine. The appendix, a small, closed tube, extends from the cecum. This tube once helped our animal ancestors digest fibrous plants. It has no known role in human digestion. The appendix does contain lymph tissue, which may help fight disease.[1] Lymph tissue is part of the **lymphatic system**, a network of vessels and organs that circulates fluid in the body and defends against infection.

Most of the large intestine is made up of the colon. This tube is divided into segments. One segment, the ascending colon, connects to the cecum and extends up the right side of the abdomen. The next segment, the transverse colon, extends across the abdomen from right to left. The descending colon travels from the transverse colon down the left side of the abdomen. An S-shaped tube called the sigmoid colon connects the descending colon to the rectum. The rectum, a tube 5 inches (12.7 centimeters) long, leads to the anal canal and the anus.

ANUS. At the very end of the digestive tract, the anal canal and the anus expel wastes from the body. Two sphincters run through the anal canal. They open to allow the wastes out of the body.

Related Organs

PANCREAS. Several nearby body parts play key roles in the digestive system. The pancreas is a gland that secretes chemicals to control the amount of **glucose** in the body. Glucose comes from the food we eat and provides energy. One of the most important pancreatic chemicals is **insulin**. The pancreas lies behind the stomach, next to the duodenum on one side and the spleen on the other. A duct, which runs through the pancreas, empties into the duodenum.

LIVER. Another important player in digestion is the liver. The largest of the body's internal organs, the liver weighs about three pounds (1.4 kilograms). It lies in the upper right part of the abdomen. The liver protects the body by extracting poisons from the blood and breaking down alcohol and other harmful substances. It produces bile, a fluid that helps break down fats.

The liver also stores **carbohydrates** and vitamins and plays a role in the excretory system. This remarkable organ performs more than five hundred tasks.[2]

GALLBLADDER. Attached to the liver, the much smaller gallbladder also serves as part of the team. Shaped like a pear, the gallbladder acts as a storage unit for the liver's bile. It can hold all the bile the liver produces in half a day.

SPHINCTERS. Sphincters separate all these organs from the digestive system. As in other parts of the system, these valves help prevent unwanted substances from leaking into areas where they could cause harm.

NERVES. The digestive system also gets help from two kinds of nerves. Extrinsic nerves come from outside the digestive system. The vagus nerves, a pair of long nerves running from the brain to the abdomen, are involved in many tasks. Intrinsic nerves lie in the walls of the digestive tract. Both types of nerves release chemicals that play a role in digestion.

Excretory System

The excretory system is made up of four different parts that rid the body of waste products. The wastes are the byproducts of chemical reactions involved in breathing, eating, and other vital activities. The four parts are the lungs, the liver, the sweat glands in the skin, and the **urinary system**, made up of two kidneys, two ureters, the urinary bladder, and the urethra. They work together to rid the body of liquid wastes and excess salts and water. They also keep the body's chemistry in balance.

LUNGS. The lungs' main function is to supply the body with oxygen. The excretory system uses the lungs to get rid of waste gases inhaled when a person breathes. The lungs resemble two large balloons, each roughly the shape of a cone. Each lung contains more than 300 million alveoli—tiny balloonlike sacs— grouped together in bunches like grapes. Gases, including oxygen and carbon dioxide, flow through the thin walls of the alveoli.

alveoli

Waste in the form of carbon dioxide flows through the thin walls of the alveoli in the lungs.

The lungs lie within the chest, in the thoracic cavity, protected from outside forces by the ribs. The right lung is divided into three parts, or lobes. The left lung, with only two lobes, is slightly smaller to make room for the heart. Each lung is enclosed in a thin, moist membrane. The lungs are among the body's most delicate organs.

SWEAT GLANDS. Sweat glands lie within the inner layer of the skin. These glands are coils of tubing surrounded by tiny blood vessels called capillaries. Wastes in the capillaries are absorbed by the sweat glands and exit through pores on the outer surface of the skin.

KIDNEYS. The human body has two kidneys. Shaped like oversized kidney beans, the two organs sit behind the stomach to the left and the right of the spine. Each kidney is about the size of a fist, 4.5 inches (about 11.5 centimeters) long, 2 to 3 inches (5 to 7.5 centimeters) wide, and slightly more than one inch (2.5 centimeters) thick. The left kidney lies slightly higher in the body and is longer and narrower than the right.

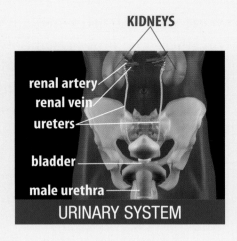

The kidneys are coated with a thin layer of tissue called the renal capsule. Beneath this, blood vessels and nerves run through each kidney. A thick layer of fat cushions the kidneys and the blood vessels. About one-quarter of the blood pumped by the heart, more than one quart (.95 liter) a minute, flows to the kidneys.[3]

Under the layer of vessels are cone-shaped structures called renal pyramids. Within the pyramids, each kidney contains about a million **nephrons**. These are made up of tiny blood vessels called capillaries covered by a membrane cap and a complex system of very small tubes called tubules. The nephrons act as tiny blood filters. The blood flows through them, leaving wastes and excess water behind. The clean fluid returns to the bloodstream.

URETER, BLADDER, AND URETHRA. A series of ducts lead from the nephrons to the ureter, a tube that drains into the bladder. The hollow bladder serves as a storage tank for urine until it is expelled through the urethra. Men and women have similar excretory systems, with the exception of the urethra. In men, the urethra is about 8 inches (20 centimeters) long. This thin tube opens into the bladder and snakes through the prostate gland and out the penis. A woman's urethra is only one fifth as long as a man's, about 1.5 inches (3.8 centimeters). It runs from the bladder to the urethral outlet.

How Do the Systems Work?

Like other body systems, the digestive system and the excretory system get their instructions from the brain. When food has to be digested or waste ejected, the brain sends an order to start the process. The order is carried by chemicals released by the **endocrine system**. This is a group of glands whose secretions help direct the body's functions. For example, the adrenal gland releases aldosterone, a chemical that helps the excretory system control how much salt is in the blood. Other chemicals help with digestion.

As the food passes through the twists and turns of the digestive tract, it is processed into smaller and smaller bits. Within this complex system, organs, fluids, glands, enzymes, and other structures work together to digest the food and send it on its way.

So efficient is a human's food-processing equipment that our bodies use almost all the food we eat. Only a small part—about

5 percent—leaves the body as waste.[1] The digestive system starts to work even before a person takes a bite. Tempting odors or tantalizing sights prompt the glands in the mouth to release saliva. This fluid contains the enzyme amylase. Amylase breaks down starchy food into sugars, which are more easily dissolved.

Hungry as a Bear

A person knows it is supper time without ever having to look at a clock. That is because the body sends out signals when it runs low on nutrients. The food we eat breaks down into glucose and other substances that fuel the body. When we have eaten a full meal, glucose stimulates nerve cells, or neurons, in the brain. These neurons turn off the brain's hunger center, located in the **hypothalamus**. The hypothalamus is a small structure at the base of the brain that controls many of the body's conditions.

The stomach can also send signals to the brain. When a big meal swells the stomach, the pressure triggers sensory neurons. They send the message that the stomach is full and that shuts off the hunger center.

After the body digests food and uses the nutrients, there is not enough glucose left to stimulate the neurons that control the hunger center. The center switches on, letting us know it is time to eat again.

Down the Hatch

When someone takes a bite of food, saliva coats the food bits chewed by the teeth. This forms a soft mass called a **bolus**. The tongue then pushes the bolus to the back of the mouth.

What happens next demonstrates once again how well the body is designed. In the throat are two tubes. One tube—the trachea—leads to the airways of the lungs. When a person breathes, air enters a small opening, called the **glottis**. The air then flows through the trachea and into the lungs. If food goes down this tube, it blocks the airflow and causes a person to choke. If the passage is not cleared quickly, the person

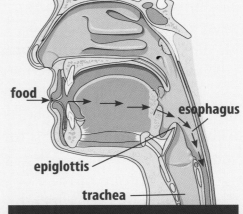

food

esophagus

epiglottis

trachea

When a person eats, the epiglottis closes off the air tube (trachea), and the food goes down the esophagus.

can die from lack of air. Food enters the second tube—the esophagus. This tube conveys food from the mouth into the stomach.

How does a person keep straight which is the air tube and which is the food tube? The body usually takes care of that without our even thinking about it. When someone swallows, a flap of cartilage called the **epiglottis** automatically seals off the glottis. With only the esophagus open, the food enters that tube and travels to the stomach. That is why we cannot take a breath at the same time we swallow. Sometimes, though, a person laughs or takes a breath while eating. That action sucks the food down the wrong tube, and it enters the trachea. Usually a person can force the food back into the mouth by coughing.

A flap of muscular fibers called the soft palate stops food from going up a person's nose. Like the epiglottis, this flap seals off the opening that leads from the nose. A person who laughs or talks while eating may force food through the opening, however.

The esophagus, with its strong muscles, works the bolus down and into the stomach. All along the esophagus, muscles contract and push the bolus forward. The wave of muscle action is called **peristalsis**.

At the bottom of the esophagus, the bolus pushes against the cardiac sphincter, which opens and lets it pass through into the stomach. The valve prevents stomach acid from flowing into the esophagus.

The vagus nerves release acetylcholine, a chemical that signals the muscles inside the digestive system to squeeze harder to force food through the tract. These nerves also stimulate the pancreas and the stomach to make more digestive juices. Another duty of the vagus nerves is to relay messages about taste from the tongue to the brain.[2]

Food stretches the walls as it passes through. This stretching action triggers the intrinsic nerves, which release a number of chemicals and other substances that either speed up or delay digestion.[3]

It Takes a Strong Stomach

The bolus travels down the esophagus to the stomach in eight seconds flat.[4] The brain has already started preparing the stomach for digestion while the food is still on the plate. Nerve cells from the brain signal the stomach to secrete gastric juice, a mix of acid, mucus, and digestive enzymes. Once food enters the stomach, gastric glands in the stomach wall release more juice.

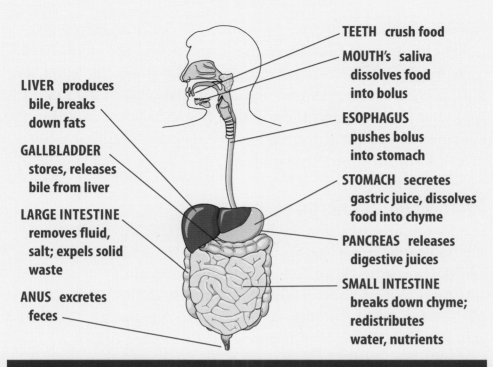

LIVER produces bile, breaks down fats

GALLBLADDER stores, releases bile from liver

LARGE INTESTINE removes fluid, salt; expels solid waste

ANUS excretes feces

TEETH crush food

MOUTH's saliva dissolves food into bolus

ESOPHAGUS pushes bolus into stomach

STOMACH secretes gastric juice, dissolves food into chyme

PANCREAS releases digestive juices

SMALL INTESTINE breaks down chyme; redistributes water, nutrients

DIGESTIVE SYSTEM TASKS

Cells in the stomach lining secrete the hormone gastrin, which also triggers the release of gastric juice.[5]

Acid in the juice kills most **bacteria** (germs) on the food we eat. The stomach also releases the enzyme pepsin, which helps break down protein. These substances would devour the stomach itself if it weren't for the thick layer of mucus that coats the stomach lining. The stomach rapidly replaces damaged cells. The lining casts off half a million cells every minute and replaces itself every three days.[6]

The upper parts of the stomach act as a storage bin for food while it waits to be digested. The muscles in the wall of the stomach churn the food into a fine pulp and mix it with gastric juice. This mixture, the consistency of a milkshake, is called **chyme**. The muscles in the stomach toss the chyme in a wave motion. The strongest muscles, in the stomach's lower section, contract several times a minute. Hormones in the pyloric sphincter that separates the stomach from the small intestine regulate the muscle action. When the stomach is full, it releases more gastrin to speed up digestion.

From Food to Energy

Even with all this action to dissolve and break down the food, the body still cannot get nutrients from chyme. It must be broken down further for it to enter the bloodstream.

After several hours in the stomach, the chyme gradually pushes through the pyloric sphincter into the duodenum. This action signals the small intestine and three other organs to begin their tasks. The small intestine releases mucus to protect against the strong stomach acid in the chyme. It also secretes hormones that tell the liver to produce bile and the gallbladder and the pancreas to add their fluids to the mix.

Bile, the thick, yellowish-green liquid made in the liver, plays a key role in the digestive system. Stored in the gallbladder, it flows through the bile duct and into the small intestine. There it mixes with chyme and makes it less acidic. The bile joins with pancreatic juices to break down fat molecules. This allows the body to absorb the vitamins that are dissolved in the fat. Without bile, the fat molecules would be too big to pass through the intestine walls, and we would not get the vitamins we need.

Enzymes from the pancreas and the small intestine break down protein into amino acids and carbohydrates into glucose. The liver changes the glucose into **glycogen**, which the liver stores for future use. Vitamins are also stored in the liver. When the body signals for more energy, the liver changes glycogen into glucose. The glucose flows into the blood, providing the body with the energy it needs. The blood also carries protein to cells throughout the body. Protein builds tissue and repairs it, helping our bodies heal. It plays a key role in fighting germs by producing antibodies.

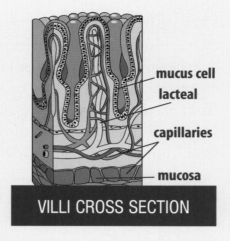

mucus cell
lacteal
capillaries
mucosa

VILLI CROSS SECTION

Bacteria in the small intestine help break apart the particles in chyme. Muscles in the small intestine contract several times a minute. The contractions go back and forth along the length of the intestine. This mixes the chyme with enzymes, bile, and juices.

Twenty thousand tiny villi line the intestine's walls. Like plants under water, the villi sway back and forth. This action sweeps fats and nutrients close to the villi. Even smaller micro-villi release enzymes that mix with enzymes from the pancreas to break down the nutrients into molecules.

Capillaries in the villi absorb the nutrient molecules, glucose, and amino acids and carry them to the liver. Most of the water enters the bloodstream. A lymphatic vessel called a lacteal extends down the center of each villus and carries fat to lymph ducts.

At day's end, the small intestine—with help from the liver, the pancreas, and the gallbladder—has processed about 2.5 gallons (9.5 liters) of food, water, and other fluids.[7]

Out With the Bad

By the time the small intestine has finished its work, there is little left of that apple or cheeseburger. A wave of muscles sends the used-up chyme on the last leg of its journey. It pushes through the ileocecal valve and into the large intestine. The large intestine has two main jobs. It must remove fluids and salts from the material that comes from the small intestine, and it must eject the solid waste that remains.

Chyme enters the colon through the cecum at the body's lower right side. It travels up the ascending colon, across the transverse colon, and down the descending colon. Then it enters the sigmoid colon and travels into the rectum.

Billions of bacteria live in the colon. They feed off waste products in the intestines and digest the last particles in the chyme. These bacteria produce vitamins, folic acid, and other substances the body uses. They also create methane and other gases that may have a bad odor when expelled.

As the chyme and fluid travel up and around the large intestine, the liquid seeps through the walls of the colon. Between one and two liters of liquid enter the colon each day.[8] Almost all of that is returned to the body. The solid matter left from the chyme is called feces.

How would you like a job where you worked only once or twice a day? That is what the rectum does. Usually it stays empty with nothing to do. The colon's muscles contract to push the feces out. When the feces reach the rectum, the mass presses on nerve cells there. These alert the spinal cord, which signals the rectum's muscles to contract. This forces the feces through the anus and outside the body. The urge to push the feces out is called the **defecation reflex**.

A WORD ABOUT BACTERIA[9]

Bacteria—billions of them—live in our intestines and help keep us healthy. These tiny, one-celled creatures help digest our food and supply us with necessary vitamins.

As in most other things, however, there are good bacteria and bad bacteria. Even different strains of bacteria in the same family can have opposite effects on us. For example, *E. coli* bacteria live in the intestines and provide vitamins K and B complex. But a certain strain of *E. coli* can be deadly. That is because these *E. coli* bacteria carry a virus and produce a poison that damages the intestines. As a result, a person infected with the bacteria may have diarrhea and lose water and salts. The person's blood vessels may also be damaged, causing bleeding. Small children are at risk because they cannot survive the loss of much water and blood.

Deadly strains of *E. coli* have been found in beef, unpasteurized apple juice, vegetables, and other foods. People can reduce the chances of being infected by *E. coli* by washing fruits and vegetables, buying pasteurized milk and apple juice, cooking meats thoroughly, washing hands, and keeping cooking surfaces clean.

Humans may not always want to respond immediately to the reflex. A person may be in the middle of a meeting or at a spot without a bathroom nearby. Special equipment in the rectum comes to the rescue. Two sphincters in the anus must open to let the feces out. The internal anal sphincter is an **involuntary muscle** that opens and closes automatically. A person can control the external anal sphincter. By telling the valve not to open, a person can delay defecation.

Excretory System at Work

The heart pumps about a quart (about a liter) of blood into the kidneys every minute. The kidneys' job is to remove everything from the blood except cells and proteins and then use the tubules to collect what the body needs: water, the right mix of salts, and nutrients. The waste and toxins, mixed with a small amount of water, are expelled as urine.

The nephrons in the kidneys act as tiny blood filters. Blood entering the kidneys flows into the glomerulus, a mass of capillaries shaped into a ball. Liquid is absorbed through the thin walls of the capillaries into the membrane of a cuplike section of tubing called Bowman's capsule. From there, the fluid travels through the renal tubules and empties into the collecting tube.

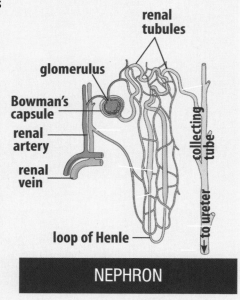

renal tubules
glomerulus
Bowman's capsule
renal artery
renal vein
loop of Henle
collecting tube
to ureter

NEPHRON

Blood vessels surrounding the nephrons absorb the filtered blood and return it to the body. Nutrients, salts, and water also are returned to the body. A small amount of waste liquids leave the body in sweat.

Most of the waste liquid continues on through the tubing to a U-shaped section called the loop of Henle. Salt around the loop of Henle draws out much of the remaining water. The rest of the liquid waste—urine—then enters the collecting tube and travels through the ureters to the bladder.

When the bladder contains about sixteen ounces (almost half a liter) of urine, sensors in the bladder walls signal the brain. The nervous system sends an order to the muscles in the bladder to contract, forcing the urine out of the bladder. In the sphincter another muscle, which blocks off the urethra, relaxes and the urine flows out. Like the rectum, the urethra can be controlled by a **voluntary muscle** that allows a person to delay urinating.

In addition to its role in the digestive system, the liver assists the excretory system by breaking down proteins and other compounds. The waste from this process, in the form of urea, leaves the body in the urine and sweat. Urea is a compound containing nitrogen.

A small amount of water, salts, and urea from the liver travels through the blood to the sweat glands. When the body is hot, the mixture travels through the gland's tubing and exits through an opening on the skin called a pore. This not only rids the body of waste but also helps keep it cool.

The excretory system also works with the **respiratory system** to expel carbon dioxide from the lungs. This waste gas is created when the body uses oxygen to produce energy. Once inhaled, oxygen passes into the alveoli and then diffuses through the capillaries into the blood that the heart pumps through the arteries to the body's parts. Most of the carbon dioxide dissolves in the blood to form bicarbonate. This helps keep the blood from becoming too acidic or too alkaline. This bicarbonate is carried by the blood through the veins to the lungs. There it is changed back into carbon dioxide and exhaled by the lungs when a person breathes out.

Balancing Act

The excretory system is part of a team that helps keep the internal body well balanced and healthy. This delicate balancing act is called homeostasis. It ensures that the body stays at just the right temperature, has just enough but not too much water and salt, and receives the exact amount of oxygen it needs. This process tells the body when it needs to sleep, drink more water, or take a breath.

The hypothalamus serves as the central command of the team. It acts like a thermostat that keeps the house warm. When the temperature in the room begins to cool, the sensors in the thermostat tell the furnace to turn on, bringing more heat to the house.

The body systems work in a similar way. When the body needs more water, for example, receptors in the hypothalamus detect the situation. The hypothalamus then sends orders to the excretory system to reduce the amount of water expelled in the urine. That is why urine looks bright yellow when a person has not drunk enough fluids. The digestive system also receives an order—to drink more fluids.

Two hormones—aldosterone and antidiuretic hormone (ADH)—help the excretory system maintain the right balance between salt and water in the blood. Aldosterone helps the body retain salt, while ADH helps the body absorb more water. When a person eats a salty meal or has too much salt in the system, the brain releases less aldosterone. When a person drinks too little water, more ADH is produced.

Disease and Disorders

The digestive and the excretory systems are so complex that many things can go wrong. If only one part breaks down, it can throw off the entire process. The stomach's digestive juice contains acids strong enough to dissolve iron nails. Potent bacteria are part of the systems. Uncontrolled, these substances can cause major health problems. In fact, digestive problems top the list of disorders that lead to surgery, hospitalization, and disability.[1]

Stomachaches and Pains

When food, drink, or germs irritate the stomach, the stomach muscles may push the offending material up through the cardiac sphincter. This causes a person to vomit. Medicines can soothe the irritation. But the best advice is to avoid such irritants and to wash and prepare food properly.

Sometimes stomach acid leaks into the esophagus. This causes a burning sensation called heartburn, although the heart is not involved. The technical name for the disorder is gastroesophageal reflux disease (GERD). The discomfort usually goes away by itself.

But if enough acid leaks into the esophagus, it can eat away tissue. Pregnancy, certain foods, being overweight, and the use of alcohol and tobacco may lead to GERD, but doctors are not certain of its cause. Medicines can reduce the amount of acid in the stomach. Surgery may be needed if too much tissue is damaged.

Ulcers

Ulcers affect about 10 percent of people living in developed countries.[2] Mucus-secreting cells protect the stomach from the harsh acids that break down food. Scientists believe the bacterium *Helicobacter pylori* may break through the mucus layer. This allows stomach acid to destroy tissue in the stomach lining. The result is an ulcer. Antibiotics—medicines that fight bacteria—are used to treat ulcers. Surgery may be required to repair scar tissue or a hole in the stomach wall.

Inflammatory Bowel Disease

Inflammatory bowel disease (IBD) refers to a group of illnesses that cause the intestines to become inflamed. Crohn's disease is one form of IBD that may affect as many as one million Americans.[3] It can damage the small or large intestine or the stomach lining and cause swelling that blocks the passages that expel waste. Researchers believe Crohn's disease may result from the immune system's reaction to a virus or bacterium. There is no cure, but medications can help ease symptoms. About one third of those with Crohn's may require surgery to remove the damaged section of the intestines, parts or all of the stomach, or the entire colon.[4] A person whose stomach is removed has to eat a special diet and take medications to help with digestion. When the colon is removed (colectomy), a tube carries the waste from the small intestine to a bag attached outside the abdomen.

Diverticular Disease

Sometimes people have to strain to push out feces that are hard and dry. If this happens too often, it can push a small section of the colon lining through weak spots in the muscle wall. Feces and bacteria become trapped in these small pockets, called diverticula, causing tissue to become inflamed. This condition, diverticular disease, can be painful and can cause fever. Antibiotics help kill the bacteria causing the inflammation.

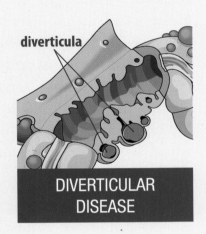

diverticula

DIVERTICULAR DISEASE

Liver Disease

An estimated 30,000 people die each year from liver disease, or **cirrhosis**.[5] In cirrhosis, liver cells become damaged and bands of scar tissue form. This prevents the liver from doing its job. Cirrhosis can result from drinking too much alcohol or from hepatitis, a disease caused by a virus. Poisons in the environment, some medications, and blocked bile ducts can also cause cirrhosis. Sometimes doctors can replace a damaged liver with a healthy liver transplanted from a person who has died. Less often, a piece of liver from a living donor has been used to replace a diseased liver.

Kidney Disease

Like the liver, the kidneys filter out harmful substances. They, too, can be damaged beyond repair. Poisons swallowed or inhaled can damage kidneys quickly. Usually, though, other diseases such as diabetes and high blood pressure gradually cause kidneys to fail. These disorders damage the kidneys' nephrons and prevent them from filtering harmful substances. Like livers, kidneys can be transplanted from a person who has died. Or a healthy person, usually a family member, may donate one kidney to the sick person. People can live quite well with only one kidney. A machine that filters the blood can be used on people whose kidneys have failed. This process is called **dialysis**.

Cancer

Cancer can attack almost any area of the body, including the digestive and the excretory systems. In a healthy person, cells grow and divide, creating new cells as they are needed. Cancer causes the cells to divide and increase out of control. The extra cells form a growth, or tumor, that can take over other parts of the body, destroying tissue and organs.

Colorectal cancer has declined in the United States, but it remains the second most deadly form of cancer.[6] Drug treatments called chemotherapy can stop some cancers. Another treatment kills cancer cells with radiation. Often surgery is needed to remove tumors.

Staying Healthy

Unhealthy habits and a poor diet cause most of the problems people have with the digestive and the excretory systems. Smoking and heavy alcohol use put people at risk for cancer. Too much alcohol harms the liver. Overeating taxes the stomach and the intestines and leads to obesity.

We Are What We Eat

The foods we eat provide the ingredients for a healthy body. Organs, muscles, and some chemicals in the body are made of protein. Protein is found in meat, fish, eggs, beans, nuts, and dairy products.

Carbohydrates—sugars and starches—provide fuel for the body. Simple carbohydrates come from sugar, fruits, and sweets and are absorbed quickly. Complex carbohydrates, from vegetables, bread, and pasta, stay in the body longer. They are converted to glycogen and stored in the liver and the muscles until needed. Some carbohydrates cannot be easily digested, but the body can still use them. For example, tough celery stalks and other fiber help form feces and make it easier to expel waste. Fluids also help this process.

Our bodies use fat as well as carbohydrates for energy. Fats and oils are needed to make cell membrane and some hormones. They also act as storage units for essential vitamins. But certain fats can clog blood flow or lead to obesity.

Diet and Exercise

The food we eat gives us energy to do the activities we want to do. **Calories** measure the energy food provides. We need calories to breathe, to circulate the blood in our veins, and even to digest food. Activities such as running and walking use up more calories.

Foods high in fat are also high in calories. For example, a medium order of french fries from a fast-food

Exercise uses up extra calories and helps us keep fit and trim.

restaurant contains 360 calories, while a medium-size baked potato with skin has only about 163 calories. Add a pat of butter (about 1.5 teaspoons or 7 grams), and the calorie count increases to 199.

Our bodies can use only so many calories at a time. If we eat more calories than we use, the calories are stored as fat. Too much fat leads to obesity and its related health problems.

A person who is not very active may only need 2,000 calories a day to fuel the body. A professional athlete may need more than 6,000 calories a day. Exercise can help keep us trim because it uses up a good portion of the calories we eat.

Stress and Its Effects

Emotions affect digestion. That was proven in 1833 when a young soldier developed a hole in his stomach after being shot. Doctors viewing the soldier's stomach through the hole saw that it made less gastric juice when he was afraid.

Later research found that the body stops digesting food when it needs to respond to fear, anger, or other strong emotion. Strong emotions trigger the release of adrenaline. This hormone puts the body on alert. But it also signals the muscles in the digestive tract to stop contracting. Food speeds through the intestines before water and nutrients can be absorbed. Diarrhea or other health problems may result.

Checkups

Doctors use high-tech tools to find cancers in the colon and other areas of the digestive tract before they spread to different parts of the body. An endoscope allows doctors to see inside the colon, the esophagus, and other areas. An endoscope is a long, thin tube with a light and a camera at the end. Regular screenings for colorectal cancer after age fifty have been shown to reduce the number of deaths from the disease.[1] Urine and blood tests can detect infections or other problems in the excretory system.

Keeping the Tract on Track

Most of the time the digestive and the excretory systems take whatever food we toss their way and process it without complaint. This marvelous machinery chugs along without a thought from us. Usually we think about digestion and excretion only when we have a problem.

Food plays a vital role in our lives. Without these systems, however, food would do us no good. That is why it is important to keep these incredible systems operating smoothly. Eating a healthy diet, exercising, getting checkups, and avoiding stress help keep the digestive tract on track.

Getting regular checkups and tests helps determine whether your body systems are working properly.

36

Amazing but True

Most people retain some alcohol in the blood up to two to three hours after a single drink.[1]

It takes about six weeks for a person's liver to grow back to normal size after more than half of the organ is removed for a transplant operation.[2]

Cells that line the stomach are constantly being shed and replaced. The stomach casts off up to half a million cells a minute. New cells take their place.[3]

If stretched out, the villi in your small intestine would cover an area the size of a football field (about 5,400 square yards). The villi cover 150 times the surface occupied by the skin.[4]

VILLI

A person who has advanced liver disease will have yellow skin. This is caused when old red cells that are usually destroyed by the liver break down and remain in the bloodstream.

Some body parts do their jobs more quickly than others. The esophagus transports food from the mouth to the stomach in about eight seconds.[5]

It takes the stomach one to three hours to digest food. Food passes through the small intestine in about four hours. The large intestine may take up to forty-eight hours to complete its food-processing job.

The liver produces up to a quart (about a liter) of bile every day.[6]

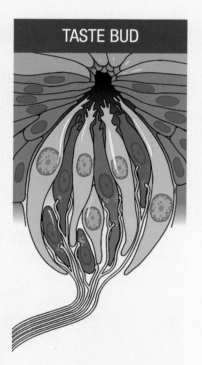

TASTE BUD

Babies have taste buds all over their mouths. Adults have far fewer taste buds—about ten thousand taste buds—and they are found mostly on the tongue. That is why babies don't like strong flavors, and adults usually prefer a variety of spices and foods.[7]

An average person produces about 10,000 gallons (almost 38,000 liters) of saliva during a lifetime.[8]

Scientists have found kidney stones in a 7,000-year-old mummy.

Made of crystals of urine that form inside the kidney, kidney stones still annoy us today. They usually can be disposed of by drinking water and ejecting them through the urine. Doctors may use shock waves to break apart large stones.[9]

The stomach lining consists of about 35 million glands that produce two to three pints (about 1.5 liters) of gastric juice every day.[10]

Ten billion microvilli can be found in just one square inch (6.5 square centimeters) of the small intestine.[11]

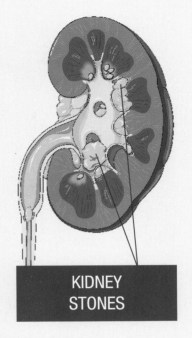

KIDNEY STONES

Urine is sterile when released from a healthy body. It becomes contaminated by germs only after being exposed to the outside environment.

Astronauts are more likely than earthbound folks to develop kidney stones while in space or shortly after a space trip. Space travel reduces a person's urine output and increases the amounts of calcium, phosphate, and sodium expelled through the urinary tract.

Chapter Notes

Chapter One: What Are the Digestive and Excretory Systems?

1. "How Your Kidneys Work," National Kidney Foundation, n.d., <http://www.kidney.org/kidneydisease/howkidneyswrk.cfm> (January 20, 2012).
2. "Feces," Encyclopædia Britannica, n.d., <http://www.britannica.com/EBchecked/topic/203293/feces>. (January 20, 2012).

Chapter Two: Members of the Team

1. Mark Galan, *Human Body* (New York: Time Life Inc., 1992), p. 90.
2. Alma E. Guinness, *ABCs of the Human Body* (Pleasantville, N.Y.: The Reader's Digest Association, Inc., 1987), p. 244.
3. George Zuidema, M.D., ed., *The Johns Hopkins Atlas of Human Functional Anatomy* (Baltimore, Md.: Johns Hopkins University Press, 1997), p. 149.

Chapter Three: How Do the Systems Work?

1. Alma E. Guinness, *ABCs of the Human Body* (Pleasantville, N.Y.: The Reader's Digest Association, Inc., 1987), p. 250.
2. Henry Gray, "The Vagus Nerve," *Anatomy of the Human Body*, 19 <http://www.bartleby.com/107/205.html> (January 20, 2012).
3. "Your Digestive System and How It Works," National Digestive Diseases Information Clearinghouse, n.d., <http://digestive.niddk.nih.gov/ddiseases/pubs/yrdd/>. (January 20, 2012).
4. *Innerbody*, HowToMedia, Inc., 1999–2011, <http://www.innerbody.com/htm/body.html>. (January 23, 2012).
5. Charles Clayman, M.D., ed., *The Human Body: An Illustrated Guide to Its Structure, Function and Disorders* (New York: DK Publishing Inc., 1995), p. 158.
6. Guinness, p. 242.
7. Ibid., p. 248.
8. George Zuidema, M.D., ed., *The Johns Hopkins Atlas of Human Functional Anatomy* (Baltimore, Md.: Johns Hopkins University Press, 1997), p. 135.
9. John C. Brown, "What the Heck is an E. coli?" Department of Molecular Biosciences, University of Kansas, 1997, <http://people.ku.edu/~jbrown/ecoli.html> (January 23, 2012).

Chapter Four: Disease and Disorders

1. "Digestive Diseases and Nutrition" (Bethesda, Md.: National Institute of Diabetes & Digestive & Kidney Diseases, 2001), p. 55.

2. Charles Clayman, M.D., ed., *The Human Body: An Illustrated Guide to Its Structure, Function and Disorders* (New York: DK Publishing Inc., 1995), p. 165.

3. Joan Gomez, M.D., *Positive Options for Crohn's Disease* (Alameda, Calif.: Hunter House Inc., 2000), p. 168.

4. "Digestive Diseases and Nutrition," p. 69.

5. "Liver Cirrhosis Mortality in the United States, 1970–2007," National Institute on Alcohol Abuse and Alcoholism, Surveillance Report #88, August 2010. <http://pubs.niaaa. nih.gov/publications/surveillance88/Cirr07.htm> (January 23, 2012).

6. "Colorectal Cancer Statistics," Centers for Disease Control and Prevention, n.d., <http://www.cdc.gov/cancer/colorectal/ statistics/index.htm> (January 23, 2012).

Chapter Five: Staying Healthy

1. "Frequently Asked Questions About Colorectal Cancer," Centers for Disease Control and Prevention, n.d., <http:// www.cdc.gov/cancer/colorectal/basic_info/faq.htm#6> (January 23, 2012).

Chapter Six: Amazing but True

1. "Nutrition and Your Health: Dietary Guidelines for Americans," Fourth Edition, Home and Garden Bulletin No. 232, U.S. Department of Agriculture, 1995.

2. "Man Donates Over Half of his Liver to his Sister in UM Medical Center's First Living Donor Liver Transplant," *University of Maryland Medical News*, October 20, 1999.

3. Mark Galan, *Human Body* (New York: Time Life Inc., 1992), p. 94.
4. Ibid., p. 88.
5. *Innerbody*, HowToMedia, Inc., 1999–2011, <http://www.innerbody.com/text/foodtrv.html> (January 23, 2012).
6. *Innerbody*.
7. Galan, p. 119.
8. Ibid., p. 82.
9. "Kidney Stones in Adults," National Kidney and Urologic Diseases Information Clearinghouse, NIH Publication No. 00-2495, February 2000.
10. *Innerbody*.
11. Robert D. Fusco, M.D., "Celiac Sprue," Three Rivers Endoscopy Center, 1997, <http://www.gihealth.com/html/education/celiacspruearticle.html> (January 23, 2012).

Glossary

bacteria—Tiny, one-celled organisms; some cause disease in the human body.

bile—Substance produced by the liver that helps break down fats.

bolus—Soft ball of food.

calories—The measure of energy provided by food.

carbohydrates—Sugars and starches that provide fuel for the body.

chyme—Watery mixture of food and gastric juice.

cirrhosis—Liver disease.

defecation reflex—The urge to have a bowel movement.

dialysis—A mechanical process that separates wastes from blood and fluid; used when kidneys fail.

digestive tract—A long tube that runs from the mouth to the anus.

endocrine system—A collection of glands that release chemicals into the bloodstream.

enzymes—Proteins that help break down food and speed chemical reactions.

epiglottis—A flap of cartilage that covers the glottis to allow a person to swallow.

gland—An organ that makes a certain substance and releases it when needed.

glottis—Opening between the mouth and the larynx through which air passes.

glucose—A sugar that supplies the body with energy.

glycogen—A substance created from glucose that stores energy.

hormones—Chemicals secreted into the body that carry messages from one part of the body to another.

hypothalamus—Small structure in the base of the brain that controls many of the body's functions.

insulin—A pancreatic hormone that regulates the levels of glucose in the blood.

involuntary muscles—Muscles that operate on their own without a person's instructions.

lymphatic system—A network of vessels and organs that carries fluid to the body and helps fight infection.

mucus—A thick liquid that coats and protects the digestive system and other body parts.

nephrons—Tiny structures in the kidneys that filter blood.

peristalsis—Wavelike motion caused when muscles relax and contract in sequence.

proteins—Molecules present in all living things that repair tissue and promote growth.

respiratory system—The body system that regulates breathing and the delivery of oxygen to the blood.

saliva—Watery substance in the mouth that softens food.

serosa—Outer layer of tissue that protects various organs.

sphincters—Bands of muscles that act like valves and close off one section of the body from another.

ulcer—An area of damaged tissue.

urinary system—A group of body parts—kidneys, ureters, urethra, and bladder—that filter liquid and rid the body of urine and liquid wastes; part of the excretory system.

villi—Tiny structures that extend into the intestines and help absorb nutrients.

voluntary muscles—Muscles that respond to a person's command.

Further Reading

Books

Burnstein, John. *The Dynamic Digestive System: How Does My Stomach Work?* New York: Crabtree Pub., 2009.

Hoffmann, Gretchen. *Digestive System*. New York: Marshall Cavendish Benchmark, 2009.

Jakab, Cheryl. *The Digestive System*. North Mankato, Minn.: Smart Apple, 2006.

Simon, Seymour. *Guts: Our Digestive System*. New York: HarperCollins, 2005.

Internet Addresses

Discovery.com. *Your Gross & Cool Body*.
<http://www.yucky.discovery.com/body>

Nemours. *KidsHealth*.
<http://www.kidshealth.org>

Index